Published by Simply Being
www.simplybeing.co.uk

Text: James Low, based on the *Padma bKa'-Thang* by Padmasambhava and *revealed* by Urgyen gLing-Pa

© James Low 2021

For the full translation of the original Tibetan text see *Facet 4, Getting Lost Invites Trouble in This Is It*, James Low, Simply Being 2020.

Illustrated by: Diana Collins. © Diana Collins 2021

Book layout and design: Hugh Johnston

ISBN: 978-0-9569239-8-1

Dedication

You who believe
that darkness is light
that might is right
Please turn to the truth
and cease to fight

Deep in the woods there are many paths leading from the clearing where we live ...

Will we choose the one that leads to true freedom?

Long, long ago in the land called Vanquished Demons there lived a spoilt young man called Masterful ...

... who had a servant called Available.

They heard of a monk called Resolute who wore the robes of renunciation yet who saw that all beings were actually buddhas.

Masterful asked around, "Is it true that Resolute shows how to be free without giving up what is bad or having to always be good? Does he say that we can do whatever makes us happy?" Everyone said, "Yes."

So Masterful set off with Available to receive these teachings. Firstly they became monks with Masterful being renamed Black Liberation and his servant was renamed Excellent. They made offerings and requested teachings.

Resolute taught them, "The basis of all you experience is your simple presence, pure and uncontrived. Rest in your unchanging open awareness and all limitations will vanish like clouds fading into the sky."

Returning home they tried to live what they had heard.

Black Liberation had listened with his ego and not his heart and so his mind remained veiled. Ignoring the open sky of his awareness he identified with the clouds of whatever impulse arose.

His dulling assumptions shrouded him in darkness while his jealousy swirled in a storm around the rock of his pride. Hot with a tidal wave of desire he became incandescent with anger whenever he was thwarted.

Excellent, the humble servant had listened carefully with his heart. He relaxed and released his reliance on his habits, thoughts and feelings. He observed how they arose and passed. His mind opened like the sky and his awareness was undisturbed by the fleeting clouds of experience.

This difference between them was obvious. Black Liberation was busy increasing the intensity of his own thoughts and feelings …

... while Excellent was relaxed and at ease with whatever occurred.

Black Liberation insisted,

"Habits and wisdom come from the same mind so they are the same. We are naturally pure so trying to be good cannot lead to liberation.

Free of plans and effort we can do as we please each moment."

Excellent replied,

"Awakening to the ungraspable source purifies both grasper and grasped. By staying present with how this is, our body, voice and mind are freed from egoic delusion."

Black Liberation insisted that Resolute confirm that he was right, but instead the teacher said,

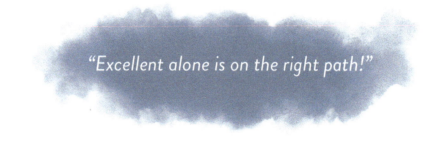
"Excellent alone is on the right path!"

At that Black Liberation became furious ...

... and drove them from the land.

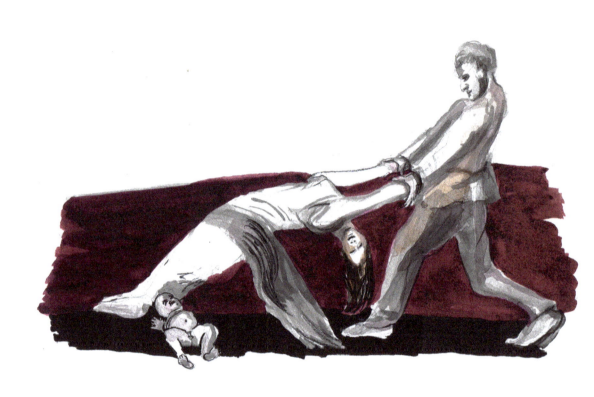

Without control or guidance Black Liberation was free to do as he pleased, confident that he was fulfilling the teachings. Self-intoxicated he killed all the men he met and took all their women.

Wild and reckless he ate human corpses in the charnel ground and dressed in human skins. After twenty long years of creating misery and havoc he suddenly died.

The ripening of his evil deeds led to 500 births each as a black wolf, as a forest rodent, as a hunting dog, as a wasp, as a maggot and as a dung eater. This was followed by 50,000 years in the lowest hell ...

... and then 20,000 years as a huge sea monster.

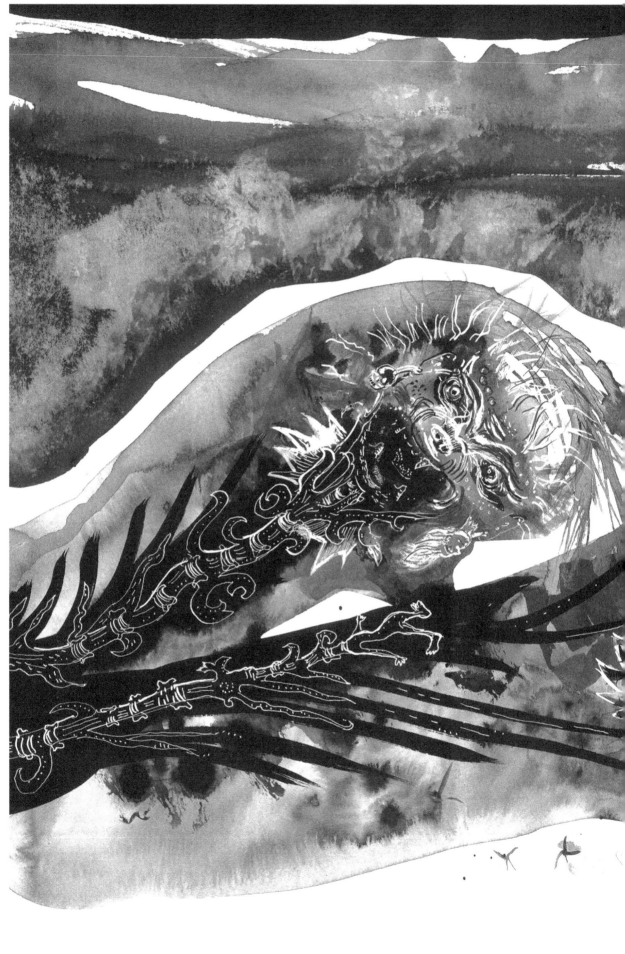

Finally he entered the womb of a prostitute who had slept with three kinds of demon that same night. Born after eight months as a small boy he had three heads each with three eyes: the central head was dark blue, the right was white and the left was red. His body was black in colour, with six hands, four legs and two wings. He was truly frightening to behold.

His birth brought misfortune to the land: criminals flooded in and sickness and sorrow multiplied.

Diseases spread and crops failed as hopelessness and despair filled the hearts of the good.

His mother died nine days after the birth and he was taken with her to the charnel ground. They were dumped beneath a huge poisonous tree named Illegitimate where the black pig of stupidity had its sty at the root,

the venomous snake of anger was coiled around the middle of its trunk, and the cockerel of desire nested at its top. The boy began to devour his mother's corpse, sucking pus and then blood from her breasts. He ate her breasts, her innards, her flesh, bones, brain and everything that remained.

Energised by this he moved around eating other corpses and drinking their blood from a skull.

Draped with human, elephant and tiger skins, he had snakes adorning his ankles, wrists and neck. His faces glistened with fat and spots of blood and he used ash from the funeral pyre to decorate his radiant body. Angry and repulsive, his faces had gaping mouths full of fangs. His skin was coarse and covered with pigs' bristles. He wore a necklace with three strands of human heads: one strand of dried heads, one of rotting and one of fresh. His hair was long and partly tied up on his head with snakes. His fingers and toes were like the claws of a bird and whatever he grabbed, dead or alive, he stuffed in his mouth and ravenously devoured. His right hands held weapons and his left held skull cups full of blood.

His breath spread diseases and many ailments flowed from his eyes, ears, anus and urethra. He was known as demon Roaring Mother-Eater.

Mother-Eater's terrifying forces were everywhere, obliterating all opposition. He was the most fierce and had the power to defeat everyone. Confident of this, he loudly proclaimed,

"I am the Lord of the World and will defeat anyone who dares to challenge me!"

All beings were cowed by him and dulled with fear and so no rival appeared.

However, his wife, Mark of Time, said,

"In Lanka, the land of the Dangerous, the king is a disciple of Buddha Dipamkara and his fame is much greater than yours."

"No enemy can defeat him and he is always happy whether awake or asleep."

Indignant at this, pride raged within him and his body blazed with fire. Roaring like thunder, glowing sparks shot from his mouth. Assembling a huge army he flew off and fell like a meteor upon the land of Lanka.

His mindless cry,

Roaring Mother-Eater Roaring!

set the whole country trembling, shaking and quaking and all its inhabitants, the demons known as Dangerous, became alarmed and extremely frightened.

The king assembled his soldiers and sent them to fight the invaders. Roaring Mother Eater furiously faced them,

"I alone am great! Who can rival me?"

In terror the king and his army bowed down, submitted and promised to serve their new ruler.

Roaring's pride knew no limit,

*"Who could be greater than I?
Roaring Mother-Eater Roaring!"*

However his wife, Mark of Time said,

"In the land of the demigods there is one called Mahakaru who is greater than you. He has great strength and supernatural power!"

Provoked by this comment his body blazed and in a rage he flew with his troops and descended on the enemy territory. He released a great rainfall of weapons and diseases which killed the demigods.

Roaring's army ate their flesh, drank their blood, and crunched their bones.

King Mahakaru was weakened by cancer and smallpox. Roaring seized his right leg and swinging him thrice around his head

hurled him away with such force that parts of his body fell on each of the eight great charnel grounds.

The stars and the planets and all who were not killed fled seeking protection. But none could be found so they had to return to the terrifying Roaring and take refuge in him. The demigods installed Roaring and his associates in the Palace called Fresh Corpse Skull and raised his victory banner.

Roaring displayed his supernatural powers. He put the highest mountain on the top of his finger and twirled it round his head, declaiming,

"Roaring Mother-Eater Roaring! On the earth, above it and below there is none greater or more victorious than I!"

However, Mark of Time remarked to him,

"*In the Joyful Heaven surrounded by monks and nuns is the great guide, holy White Pinnacle,*

*who is consecrated and praised by buddhas and gods.
They request him to teach as he is the greatest holy one."*

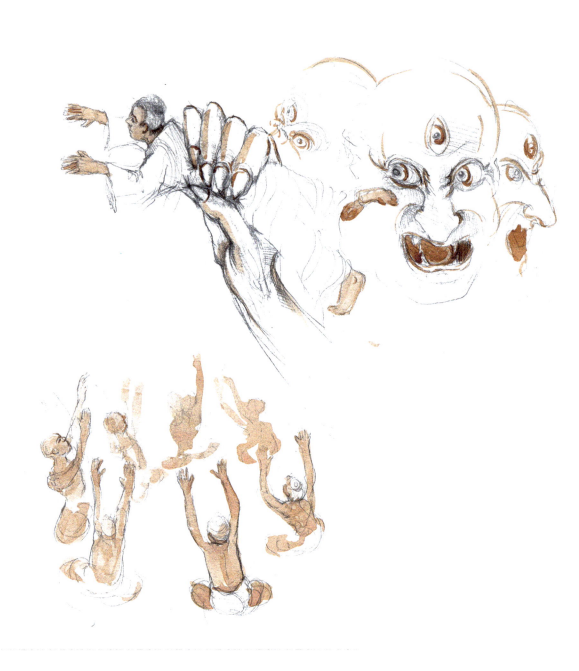

The extremely fierce and stupid Roaring became furious and snarled many insults as he flew off to Joyful Heaven. He tore holy White Pinnacle from his throne and was about to hurl him away when his followers started to wail and protest.

Roaring mocked them:

*You are half naked and sit quietly on your mats.
Why would I do what you want?!*

I AM THE SOURCE OF ALL TERROR!

Holy White Pinnacle gave his dying instructions,

"Alas my followers, Black Liberation is the disciple who broke his vows and has no faith in the dharma. Angry with the Buddha he has destroyed the world. Resolute and Excellent must quickly ripen their virtuous karma. Roaring will not be pacified or helped to flourish and so he must be overawed and destroyed. His poisonous afflictions must be transformed into liberating elixir."

"By reuniting the divided, and by liberating grasping at self, Roaring Mother-Eater, the self-cherishing of the body, will be liberated. This will also liberate Sharp Roarer, the self-cherishing of speech, source of all happiness and sorrow, and liberate Trident Roarer, the self-cherishing of the mind which generates solidification of experience. Truth and happiness will spread everywhere, and I will take birth and become Buddha Shakyamuni. Keep this prediction secret!"

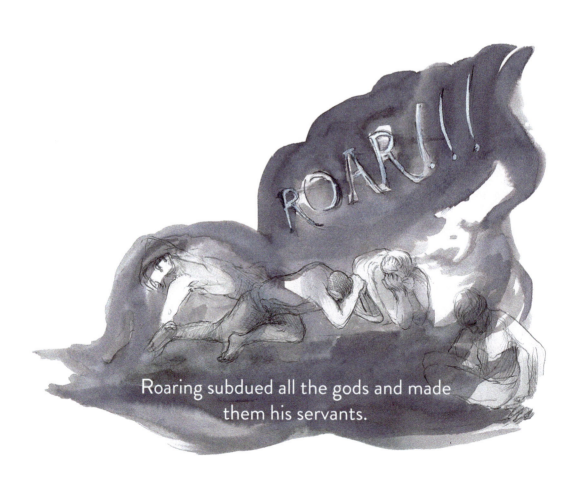

This so alarmed the great enlightened ones that they gathered to discuss what could be done. All the buddhas with all their followers arrived from every direction like a vast ocean of light and virtue.

They reached a consensus: "*If Roaring is not destroyed by the effective power of the buddhas then the pure dharma will not flourish and all beings will fall into the lower realms.*

The body performing bad actions must be attacked with the assassins' weapons. If the consequences of Roaring's activity do not ripen now then who will believe in the truth of karma? He must be completely annihilated!"

The buddhas saw with their wisdom that it was time for Resolute and Excellent to be the disciplining agents. Resolute became the buddha Indestructible Being while Excellent became bodhisattva Indestructibility.

All the buddhas and bodhisattvas manifested in front of them and gave them initiation, blessing and consecration.

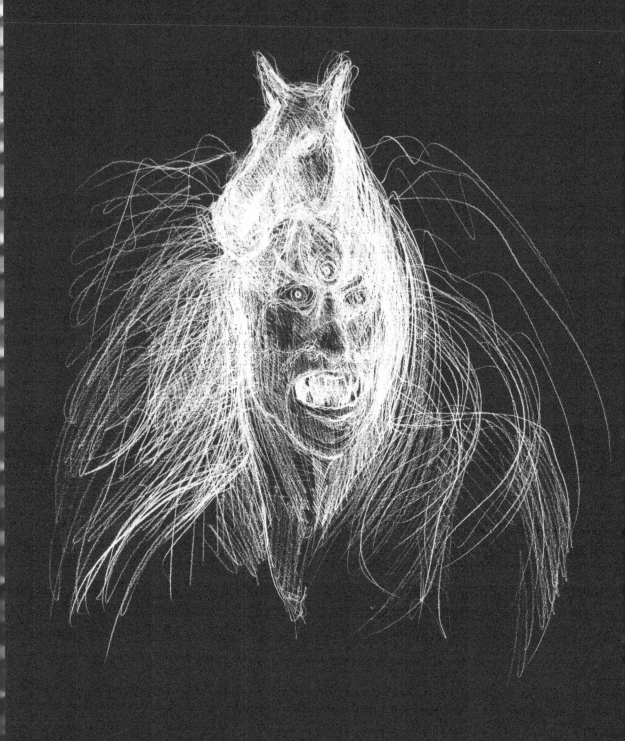

They were given their instructions and told to act accordingly: *"Resolute, you now have the compassion of the All-Seeing and the horse's head of wrathful Neighing.*

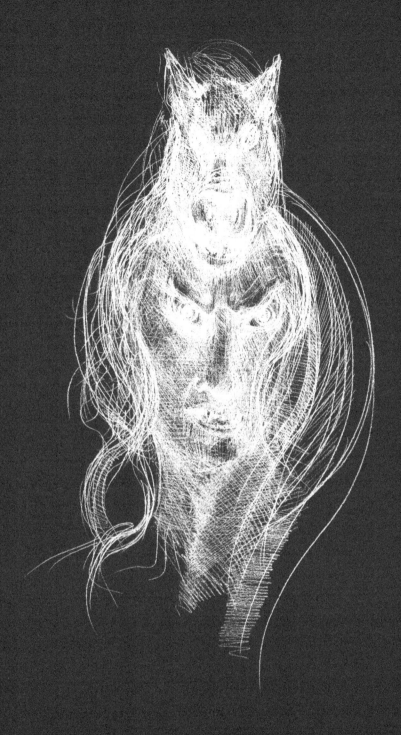

Excellent, you now have the kindness of the Saviouress and the sow's head of the Diamond Sow. We are all agreed that together you must crush Roaring — it is what must be done!"

Neighing had the form of a fierce heruka, radiant and expressing the nine moods. With his wife Diamond Sow he went to Roaring's palace on the peak of Mount Malaya. Each of the four doors had a female guard: a mare, a sow, a lioness and a bitch.

Without desire, Neighing took each of them in turn and blessed them, transforming them into the four doorkeepers: White Mare Face, Black Sow Face, Red Lioness Face and Green Bitch Face.

Entering the palace, Neighing encountered the eight female guardians who had the following heads: lioness, tigress, vixen, wolf, vulture, raptor, raven and owl.

Without desire Neighing took each of them in turn and blessed them, transforming them so they became the eight Hybrids, each a manifestation of wisdom yet retaining their predatory animal heads.

Entering further in he met the eight demonesses: Demon's Daughter, Cannibal's Daughter, Shagger, Scary, Stainless, Shriveller, Cup-Holder and Trough-Holder.

Without desire Neighing took each of them in turn, transforming them into the eight Mothers of Place, wisdom manifesting as wild demonesses.

Neighing and Diamond Sow penetrated to the heart of the palace. Roaring had gone out in search of food and so, adopting the dress and manner of Roaring, without desire Neighing took Roaring's wife Mark of Time.

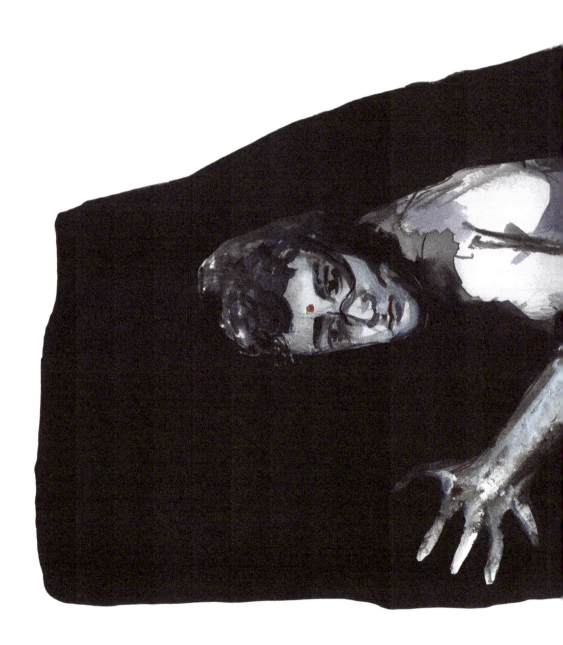

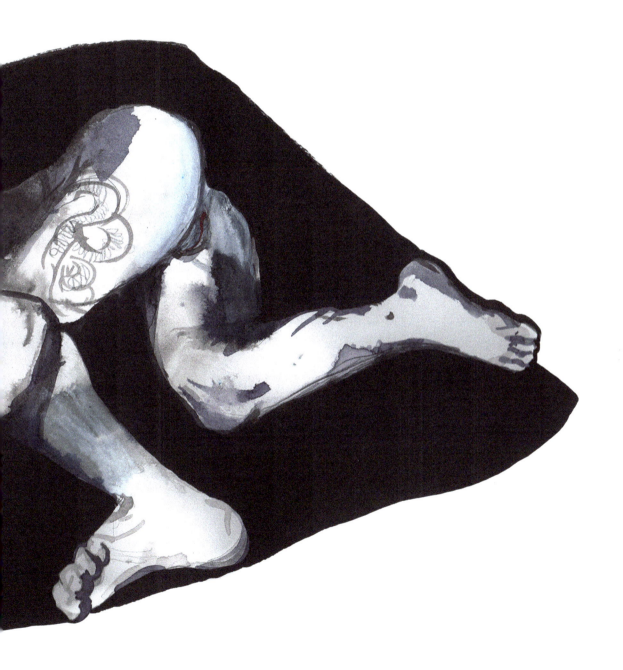

A son known as Perfect Indestructible Fierce Enlightenment was born from this with three faces, six hands and an air of vicious violence.

Neighing neighed loudly three times and his wife Diamond Sow grunted her pig sound five times. This alarmed and frightened Roaring who returned to the palace and pointing threateningly, demanded,

"What is this noise, you small people with heads of horse and sow? All the gods praise me with faith. You cannot subdue me so remain peaceful. In former times even the monks could not defeat me!"

Neighing responded by entering Roaring Black Liberation through his anus, penetrating up to the crown of his head and emerging through it. He stretched his arms and legs far apart and his horse head turned green from the boiling of Roaring's fat. His mane was dyed red with Roaring's blood, his cheeks turned yellow from Roaring's liver while a strip of white from Roaring's brain ran down his forehead and nose.

Now Roaring looked both fascinating and terrifying with these frightening adornments.

Simultaneously Diamond Sow had entered the vagina of Roaring's wife and rose up through her till her head penetrated the wife's skull. Her sow's head turned black due to the boiling of the wife's fat.

Then Neighing and Diamond Sow copulated and a son, Spotty, was born there and then.

Neighing neighed six times and Diamond Sow grunted five times and immediately the army of buddhas filled the entire sky, massing like vultures flocking towards a corpse.

Roaring Black Liberation was being stretched from within and he wept and wailed in unbearable agony, *"Father! Mother! Oh! No! Roaring has been defeated by the horse and the sow. The demons have been defeated by the buddhas. Non-virtue has been defeated by virtue. The garudas have defeated the snakes. Fire has defeated wood. Water has defeated fire. Wind has scattered the clouds. The diamond has penetrated the jewel. Yesterday's bad dream has arrived. You must kill me quickly. Do what you will!"*

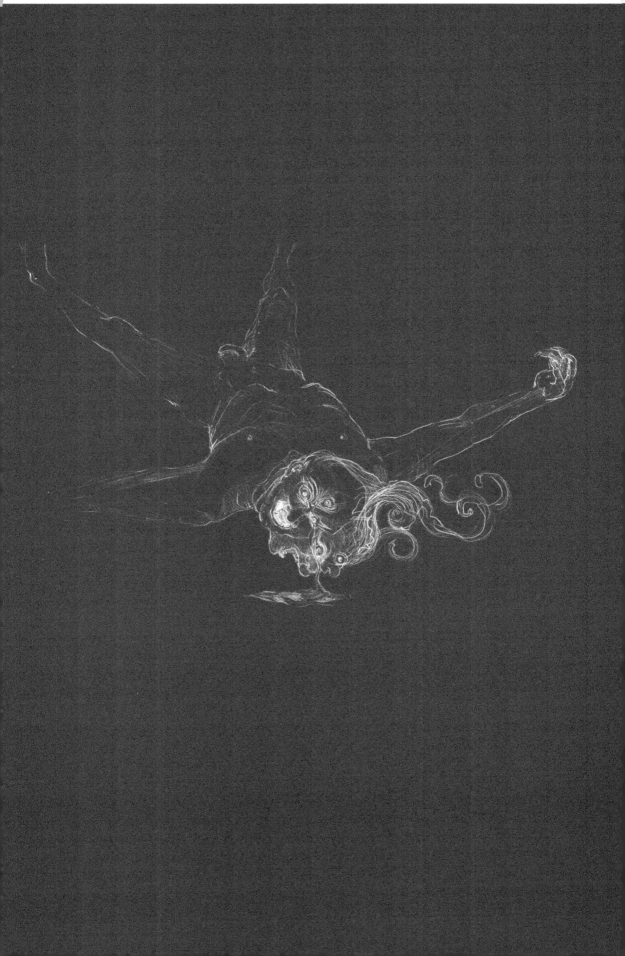

As Roaring spoke a lump of excrement came out from him and fell into the great ocean. From this arose the great wish-fulfilling tree called Sandal Essence of Snake. Its roots penetrated the land of the naga snake gods. Its leaves flourished bountifully in the land of the demigods and its fruits, known as Liberating Essence of Demon, ripened in the land of the gods.

Neighing and Diamond Sow fought but did not kill. Instead they took the enemy's dress and weapons for their own adornment. Neighing stripped Roaring and cast him out.

He blessed the eight garments and wings so that they and the nine shining expressions of mood became the manifestations of wisdom.

Bodhisattva Indestructibility and his emanations manifested in fierce forms. However, Roaring now emanated a huge and terrifying form with nine heads and eighteen hands.

Indestructibility emanated the nine wrathful forms of Heruka and countless other terrors and they completely subjugated Roaring so that his body became the palace of the buddhas and they dwelt there.

But nobody listened to his orders. His followers did not hear him or gather round for Perfect Indestructible Fierce Enlightenment had put them all under his power. All the demons and wild spirits who had followed Roaring became the close servants of Neighing. His son, Spotty, prepared offerings for the gods.

Supreme Enlightenment Indestructible Presence emanated ten Ferocious each carrying a ritual nail. They were instructed and authorised to kill Roaring and his entourage. Neighing joined them and neighed three times rendering Roaring's entire army powerless, so they meekly offered their possessions and life essence.

Bowing low they spoke humbly,

"Homage to you who are the activity of the buddhas. Salutation to you who ripen the results of karma. The result of our former bad activity is ripening as our bodies. Where we go in our next lives will be determined by our actions in this life.

Our actions follow us as our shadows follow our bodies. The karmic consequences of our actions are experienced by ourselves alone.

"We feel broken-hearted and full of regret yet we cannot alter the power of karma.

We who are tortured by our own karma offer our bodies to you as cushions. Please accept them!!"

In this way, all the enlightened Frightenings came to have male and female Roarers as their cushions.

The Lord of Secrets, Indestructibility, raised his awesome trident and pierced Roaring who fell on his back, dying.

All the sins and obscurations of his karma and afflictions were cleansed in that moment. He was given initiation, took vows and was poured the sacred water confirming these vows. His body, voice and mind were blessed and he became a dharma-protecting guardian with the secret name of Mahakala Great Black One. He was given the prediction that in a later life he would become the Buddha Powerful Dust in the realm of Effortlessly Established.

Roarer had caused so much pain and suffering but was only touched by his own misery. The peaceful healing power of the buddhas could not soften him and so they had to manifest the illusory apparitions of their terrifying potential.

The cataract of arrogant self-obsession needs to be cut free with the sharp blade of wisdom.

Praise to Hayagriva

In the red-black triangular mandala of power on top of trampled black demons, male and female, is Padma Heruka, the king of power surrounded by the fierce gods of the lotus family. We salute and praise powerful Hayagriva and his host of gods.

Praise to Dorje Phagmo

In the playful palace of the very fearful cemetery, on top of cushions of trampled, splayed out corpses is the great mother, fierce Dorje Phagmo surrounded by a retinue of diverse dangerous goddesses and dakinis. We salute and praise Dorje Phagmo and her host of deities.

Dwelling in the effortlessly arising palace called Highest, the Buddhas saw clearly how Roaring had perverted the teachings and inflicted terrible suffering on all sentient beings.

All the Buddhas then met at the pure palace called Flowing to discuss what should be done. Employing methods of pacifying, increasing, overawing and destroying they subdued the ideology of this misleading demon.

On the blazing sky iron peak of Mount Malaya the demon Roaring was finally liberated by killing. All his demon wives were enjoyed in sexual union by Heruka. Thus the first spreading of the tantric teachings arose from killing and congress.

Padmasambhava

LAST WORDS

The light is hidden by what the light reveals. We see people, trees, houses, apples. These objects hook our attention and interest. They give our thoughts and feelings something to play with. Grasping at what we like and avoiding or destroying what we do not like, we become the powerful ones who attempt to make a world of our choosing.

We are able to experience thoughts and feelings, trees and ice cream because we have a mind. What is this mind? At the start of the story, the wise and simple monk Resolute pointed out that our mind is not what we think it is. He said, "The basis of all you experience is your simple presence, pure and uncontrived. Rest in your unchanging open awareness and all limitations will vanish like clouds fading into the sky."

How surprising that the truth of our existence is our simple presence, just as it is. We open to this by resting in this moment without trying to change anything. The immediacy of the intrinsic wholeness of how we are is like the sky – open, present, hospitable, yet ungraspable and inconceivable. Thoughts tell us about thoughts. They do not reveal the open for it is the ever-open space of awareness that reveals our thoughts. Do less, receive more. Do nothing, receive all.

This story indicates how each of us is veiled and obscured by our own long-developed karmic habit formations. The spoilt young man, Masterful, had been encouraged to put himself first and to see the world in terms of his own wishes. These habits and attitudes allowed him to see the world solely in terms of himself. He was blind to his own limitations and blind to the generosity of others. "I am the boss. I say what will happen and I am always right." This imperious impervious narcissism gave him a misplaced confidence that led to his downfall.

In contrast, his servant Available was humble and curious, and so these thinner veils allowed him to receive the point of Resolute's instructions. True to his name, he became ever more open and available and so was able to open to both the infinity of his awareness and the infinity of the space of his awareness. The icicles of self-cherishing melted, and his heart glowed with goodwill for all beings.

Each of us is faced with this basic choice. Shall we turn towards the infinite potential of our instant presence, the vitality of our awareness? Or shall we turn towards the limited and limiting concerns of our ego-self? The first option brings light and love, the second brings chaos and harm.

The story presented in this book is based on an account in a Tibetan biography of the great tantric guru Padmasambhava. It is an ancient account of how the peaceful Buddhas were provoked by the destruction wrought by malicious self-indulgence into showing their wrathful potential. According to the tantric tradition, Buddhas have four main styles of activity: pacifying, increasing, overawing and fiercely dominating. When gentle kindness was not sufficient to soften the heart of Roaring, the Buddhas gathered together and authorised the display of fierce implacable virtue. The Buddhas respond to the qualities of each person and each situation. Buddhas are neither intrinsically peaceful nor wrathful – they manifest as required. This knowledge can support us in times of turmoil when it is easy to feel overwhelmed.

May the path of light open to all beings and may they find in their own heart the light to keep them on this wholesome way.